Prospecting Confidently

Prospecting
Confidently

Table Of Contents

Foreword

Have you ever felt anxious or inarticulate when speaking to a prospect? You realize the moment of truth is upon you . . . it's time to recruit this fresh prospect -- but how?

With practice this process will be easy.

Everything that happens... occurs for a reason. And from time to time, one thing leads to another. Instead of locking yourself away and weeping over preceding heartaches, embarrassment and failures, see them as your instructors and they'll become your tools in both self-improvement and success.

So, when does self-improvement turn into success? Where do we start? Take these tips in this book. Get all the info you need here.

Confident Prospecting
Building Your Prospecting Techniques In Network Marketing

Chapter 1:

Why Do We Need To Improve

Synopsis

At times, when all our questions, fears and insecurities wrap us up, we come up with the thought of "I wish I was somebody else."

More frequently than not, we think and trust that somebody or rather, most people are better than us - when actually, the fact is, a lot of people are more frightened than us.

We see a young business entrepreneur and say, "what else could he need?" He stares at himself at the mirror and grumbles to himself, "I detest my eyes... I wonder why my prospects won't talk to me...."

Isn't it curious? We look at other people, envy them for looking so terribly perfect and wish we could trade places with them, while they consider us and think of the same thing. We're jealous of other people who themselves are jealous of us. We suffer from low self-regard, lack of assurance and lose hope in self-improvement and ever winning anyone over.

The Basics

I have a friend that never gets sick of talking. And in most conversations, she's the only one who seems to be interested in the things she has to say. So all of our other friends tend to avoid her, and she doesn't notice how socially hindered she is.

One key to self-improvement is to listen and speak to a trusted friend. Find someone who is easy to open up to. Ask questions like "do you believe I'm rude?", "Do I sound argumentative?", "Do I talk too loud?", "Does my breath stink?", "Do I ever bore you?"

In that way, the other person will obviously know that you're interested in self-improvement. Listen to comments and criticisms and don't say things like "Don't exaggerate! That's simply the way I am!" Open your mind and heart too.

One of Whitney Houston's songs says, "Learning to love yourself is the greatest love of all." True! In order to love others, you have to love yourself as well. Remember, you can't give what you don't have.

Stop thinking of yourself as a second-rate being. Forget the insistent thought of "If only I was richer... if only I was thinner" and so on. Accepting your true self is the first step to self-improvement. We have to stop comparing ourselves to others.

We all have our insecurities. Nobody is perfect. We constantly wish we had better things, better features, better body parts, and so forth. But life need not to be perfect for people to be happy about themselves.

Self-improvement and loving yourself isn't a matter of crying out to the whole world that you're perfect and you're the best. It's the virtue of acceptance and contentment. Once we begin to better ourselves, we then are able to be convincing in a conversation with prospects.

Chapter 2:

Consider These Conversation Techniques

Synopsis

The opening move of having potent conversations with prospects goes on before you meet the candidate. If you've expertise in your market, tap into your insider knowledge. Otherwise, explore what motivates them.

Some Pointers

By now you ought to have a picture coming forth of who you think your 'ideal' lead is ... or who you wish it to be. Depending upon the nature of your business, you may even be able to write a description of your lead. "My target lead is a middle-class woman in her middle years who's married and has youngsters, and is environmentally conscious and physically fit." Based on the numbers you exposed in your research, above, you may even know, for instance, that there are about 9000 of those potential leads in your area! It may well be that 3000 of them are already loyal to a rival, but that still leaves 6000 who aren't, or who haven't yet bought the product from anybody. Do the research!

So how do you stay calm, composed and sustain confidence in tough surroundings? Here is some information to think about.

See yourself as a dartboard. Everything and everyone else around you may become darts, at one point or another. These darts will crush your confidence and pull you down in ways you won't even remember. Don't let them crush you, or get the best of you. So which darts should you avoid?

Dart 1: Negative Work Environment

Mind the "dog eat dog" hypothesis where everyone else is pressing simply to get ahead. This is where non-appreciative people commonly thrive. No one will value your contributions even if you miss lunch and dinner, and stay up late. Most of the time you must work too much without getting help from anybody else. Stay out of this; it will ruin your self-esteem. Competition is at stake anyplace. Be fit enough to compete, but in a levelheaded competition that is.

Dart 2: Other People's Action

Bulldozers, brown nosers, gossips, bellyachers, backstabbers, snipers, the walking wounded, controllers, naggers, bellyachers, exploders, patronizers, sluffers... all these sorts of people will pose bad vibes for your self-esteem, as well as to your confidence strategy.

Dart3: Changing Surroundings

You can't be a light-green bug in a brown field. Changes challenge our confidence. It tests our flexibility, adaptability and changes the way we think. Changes will make life hard for a while, it may cause tension but it will help us discover ways to better our selves. Change will always be around; we must be adaptable to it.

Dart 4: Past Experiences

It's all right to cry and say "ouch!" If we have pain. But don't let pain metamorphose into fear. It might grab you by the tail and swing you around. Treat each failure and error as a lesson.

Dart 5: Negative World View

Consider what you're looking at. Don't surround yourself with all the negativeness of the world. In building confidence, we have to learn how to make the best out of worst situations.

Dart 6: Purpose

The way you are and your behavioral traits is said to be a mixed end product of your genetic traits , your raising , and your environmental surroundings like your spouse, the company you keep, the economy or your occupation. You have your own individuality. If your father is a failure, it doesn't mean you have to be a failure too. Learn from others experience, so you'll never have to make the same mistakes.

Now and again, you may wonder if some people are born leaders or positive thinkers. NO. Becoming positive, and remaining positive is a choice. Building confidence and drawing lines for confidence is a choice, not a rule or a talent. God wouldn't descend from heaven and tell you - "Tom, you may now have the permission to build confidence and persuade people."

In life, it's hard to remain confident particularly when matters and individuals around you continue pulling you down. When we get to the battleground, we ought to pick out the correct weapons and armor to use, and pick those that are unassailable. Life's choices provide us more options. Along the way, we'll get hit and bruised. And wearing an unassailable armor ideally means 'self change'. The sort of change comes from inside.

Building confidence will eventually lead to self-improvement, which will lead to being able to persuade people. If we start to become responsible for who we are, what we have and what we accomplish people will take note. It's like a flame that should gradually spread like a brush fire from the inside out. When we grow self-esteem, we take charge of our mission, values and discipline. Confidence brings about self-improvement, true assessment, and determination. So how do you start setting up the building blocks of self-esteem? Be positive. Be content and happy. Be appreciative. Never miss a chance to compliment. A positive way of living will help you establish self-esteem.

A good way to begin your internal preparation is with a look at your capabilities. That means connecting with your strengths as well as your weaknesses. You'll find it truly empowering to discover, and list out, what you have to provide. It's likewise a good idea to know what your short- and long-term goals are.

As well, you need to comprehend communication, both spoken and unspoken.

A simple exercise that will help you answer these questions will likewise help you have a look inside yourself and begin to consider what you want "more of" and what you want "less of" in your life. People commonly perform at a higher level if they're fulfilled with what they do.

It's a fact: individuals are pulled to self-confident people. The reason is that it signals a high status. And we all know that individuals are highly attracted to status. The important thing here is that nearly 90 % of your approach-success depends on your body language, your tone and timing.

That means you have to dominate those areas initially. Only a strong and lucid body language will demonstrate confidence. But what does "strong and lucid body language" mean? It means that you:

1) Stand up straight.
2) Smile. You're the alpha, but you likewise have to demonstrate you're friendly.
3) Keep your shoulders and head up
4) Don't lean on the wall. A strong individual doesn't need protection.
5) Don't hold anything in front of your chest.
6) Always talk loud and clear.
7) Lean back. You're the one getting information. Never lean in.
8) Take up room. Live big.
9) Take your hands of your pockets. Instead of looking cool, it looks like you're insecure.
10) Move slowly. Never pause. Take your time.
11) Speak slowly. Your voice is a powerful weapon.

12) Look people straight in the face.

13) Don't touch your face.

14) Don't use stupid hand gestures.

15) Know how your body language resonates.

You might be surprised at how your phrasing may imply either confidence or insecurity. Many individuals version politeness with insecurity. They use words such as if, may, could, and perhaps in an effort to be polite when those words frequently ring of insecurity.

Instead, select words that send signals of confidence: when, will, would, and certainly. It's crucial that individuals get the sense that you believe in yourself. After all, if you don't, why should they? The following illustrations contrast insecure and confident styles:

Insecure: If I don't hear from you, I'll call to see if we might meet.

Confident: I'll call you next week to see when we may meet.

Insecure: I hope that you'll find my business desirable for you.

Confident: I'm confident that I may help you.

Insecure: I might be a good choice for you.

Confident: I'm the one for you.

Insecure: Hopefully we might get together to talk.

Confident: Let's meet to talk.

Insecure: Perhaps I may meet with you.

Confident: I'd like to get together with you.

Insecure: Maybe sometime next week we may find the time to meet.

Confident: Next week is a great time for me to meet with you.

Get the point? If you're tempted to utilize a word or phrase that rings of insecurity, resistant opt for the confident manner.

Showing sincerity might be a tricky thing. You need to utilize words and phrases that imply sincerity without you sounding artificial. These 7 tips will help you express sincerity:

1. It's all right to start a few sentences with I, but don't overdo it. A conversation that becomes too I-focused, is apt to draw a response like, "I, I, I! Doesn't this guy ever consider anyone except himself?"

2. Utilize concrete language. Refer to particulars you've learned, research from your own experience. If appropriate, use precise numbers, names, and places instead of generalities. For example, "I

can envision a ten percent growth in sales" is much better than "I can envision sales growth in your business."

3. Speak specifically to the prospects goals, challenges, mission statement, or anything that's relevant to the company. For example, "I'd like to be a part of opening your eyes to what you are able to accomplish."

4. Use the prospects name.

5. If you have a humorous tone throughout, break that tone from time to time with a comment like "Seriously, I know I can ..." or "Joking aside, there are a lot of issues ...."

6. Utilize an assertive (however not aggressive) tone in your closing that lets the individual know you're sincere about wanting them to sign on. For instance, "I'll contact you next week to follow up on this proposal."

7. Say thank you in a simple and honest way toward the end. Let your potential prospect know that you appreciate her attention.

Chapter 3:
Getting The Whole Picture

Synopsis

When we consider a certain object, a painting for example - we won't be able to appreciate what's in it, what is painted and what else goes with it if the painting is just an inch away from our face. Yet if we step back and consider it a bit further, we'll have a clearer vision of the entire picture.

Getting The Information You Need

Here's an example:

Try putting frog A in a pot of simmering water. What occurs? He twerps! He jumps out! Why? Because he is not able to endure sudden change in his surroundings - the water's temperature.

Then try frog B: place him in tepid water, and then turn the gas range on. Wait till the water reaches boiling. Frog B then considers "Ooh... it's a little warm in here".

Individuals are like frog B in general. Today, Lisa thinks Joe detests her. Tomorrow, Jim walks up to her and tells her he detests her. Lisa stays the same and doesn't mind what her friends say.

The following day, she learned that Kim and John also loathe her. Lisa doesn't realize the importance and the need for self-reformation till the entire community detests her.

We learn our lessons once we experience pain. We finally see the warning signs and signals when matters get harsh. When do we recognize that we have to change our diet? When none of our clothes fit us.

When do we quit eating chocolates? When all of our teeth get rotten. When do we realize that we have to quit smoking? When our lungs have broken down.

When do we pray and invite help? When we recognize that we're gonna die.

The sole time most of us ever learn about unlocking our confidence is when the whole world is crashing and crumbling. We believe and feel this way because it is not simple to change. But change becomes more atrocious when we ignore it.

Change will occur, like it or detest it. At one point or another, we're all going to experience different turning points in our life - and we're all going to sooner or later unlock our confidence not because the world says so, not because our acquaintances are nagging us, but because we recognized it's for our own good.

Happy individuals don't just accept change, they embrace it. Now, you don't have to feel an enormous pain before recognizing the need for confidence. Unlocking your confidence means letting go of the thought that "it's simply the way I am". It's such a poor excuse for individuals who fear and resist change.

Laura repeatedly tells everybody that she doesn't have the guts to be around groups of people. She heard her mom, her dad, her sister, her instructor say the same things about her to others.

Over the years, that's what Laura believes. She thinks it's her story. And what happens? Each time a crowd was in her house, in school, and in the community - she stepped back, shied away and locked herself up in a room. Laura didn't only believe in her story, she lived it.

Laura has to recognize that she is not what she is in her story. Rather than having her story absorb her life, she has to have the spirit and show individuals "I'm an important person and I ought to be treated accordingly!"

Confidence might not be everybody's favorite word, but if we see things in a different light, we may have greater chances of enjoying the whole process rather than counting the days till we're fully improved.

3 sessions in a week at the gym would result to a healthier life, reading books rather than looking at smut will shape more profound knowledge, going out with acquaintances and peers will help you take a step back from work and relax.

And just when you're enjoying the whole procedure of unlocking your confidence, you'll recognize that you're beginning to take the correct steps for speaking to prospects in the correct way.

Next is asking the right questions:

When you've introduced yourself, ask your prospect meaningful open-ended questions. Reply briefly with gratitude for them, validation for their feelings, and endorsement for their thoughts. If you begin by asking what is working well in their lives, their hardships will arise by nature.

Remember -- they're able to resolve their own issues. Resist the temptation to make suggestions unless they ask you directly. Listen and reply with understanding. Let them have the floor. Be curious.

When it's your turn to talk, be concisely enthusiastic about what you do. Weave in a short success story or two about your customers (no names) that relates to the challenges your prospect has just told you about.

We require data from others daily. Techniques we utilize to gather that data may have great impact on both its quality and quantity. Open-ended questions are not only friendlier, but they get the desired result-data- more quickly and are easier on the individual answering.

Curiously, many individuals don't know why open-ended questions are better or how to ask them, yet they may be the easiest part of conversation imaginable.

Understand the difference. An open-ended question calls for an answer greater than a single word or two. A closed-ended question may be answered with a simple "Yes," "No," or additional really simple answer.

For instance, if you wish to know what happened after you left the party, you may ask,

"Did you talk to Bob?" or
"Did Susan leave with John?" or
"Did they finish all the bubbly?"

Open ended questions are, you may simply ask "What happened after I left?" Chances are you'll hear what you wish to know somewhere in your answer. If not, you may follow that up with another open-ended question, "What happened with Susan and Jim?"

Let's say you wish to know why a date was cancelled. Was it something you had said or done? Did someone get sick? Did somebody with a pressing need call? You could ask any of these particular, closed-ended questions or the very simple and open, "Why did you cancel our date?"
If the answer was vague or too general, my next open-ended question may be just slightly less open-ended.

Me: "Why did you cancel our date?"
You: "I wasn't feeling well."
Me: "Oh? I hope you're feeling better now. What was wrong?"

After you've asked your open-ended question(s) and haven't gotten the particular information you want, it's now effective and acceptable to ask more particular questions like, "What happened to the bubbly?" A major mistake individuals make is to start with particulars, which wastes a lot of time. End with particulars, if essential.

Follow up with "Why?" or "How?" A different technique that may help you get particular information and a lengthier answer is to ask a closed-ended question followed up with "Why?" or "How?"

For instance, if I wish to know whether I might find a class useful, I may ask someone who took it.

Me: "Did you like that Sociology class?"
Him: "Nope."
Me: "Why not?"
Him: "Oh, well, it was a lot of reading and theory without much practical application, for one thing."

Be narrow and then open. If you're fighting to get the individual to open up with broad open questions, attempt narrowing the questions first and then make them broader after getting them into the conversation.

Illustration of this would be when talking to your youngsters after school and you ask, "What happened today?" "Nothing" is the response. Go to something like, "What assignment were you assigned?" Likely you'll get an answer and from this start opening up the question further.

Listen! Occasionally we're guilty of formulating the next question without attentiveness to the answer to the first. You miss excellent opportunities for follow-up questions if you do this! Make an effort to listen to the reply you asked for!

Chapter 4:

Synopsis

A particular minute may open in the conversation to enroll the prospect. Invite them to take a closer look at the business. Be ready to set up an appointment, and ask for their email and phone number so that you're able to follow up.

This part of the conversation may go something like this:

Getting Action

I understand exactly what you mean, John. What do you think it would take to make that change in your lifestyle?

Well, I've been thinking of this for years and haven't tackled it.

What would the payoff be if you achieve this today?

I'd work 20 hours less each week and have more fun in my life!

That would be grand! Is there one step you are able to take today in that direction?

Find time to produce some products to give me recurrent income.

You really know what to do; it's simply a matter of making the commitment and centering on steps. What would it mean to you if you could do this today?

It would better my family life for one.

You're talking about things that are close to my heart. As a matter of fact, my specialty is supporting entrepreneurs to produce a lifestyle driven business rather than a business driven life-style.

Really? How do you achieve that?

We'd start by developing a complete vision for your new lifestyle, then we'd set incremental milestones. With what you've told me I believe it would be possible for you to free up time, expand your income streams and meet many of your life-style goals by the end of this year.

I truly do need to do this. I've been suffering with this for too long.

I hear that. Let's sit down and arrange a plan . . .

Notice that it's not even necessary to mention a certain business, which removes the obstacle of having to define what the business is. If the prospect isn't ready to take a step with you now, ask if they'd like to sign up for your free e-zine/report/blog so that you're able to continue to contact them. Or, invite them to your upcoming event, -- workshop or tele-class and so on.

If you do everything beautifully up to this point and then miss the ball here, it might cost you all the effort that's gone before. Always follow up within twenty-four hours or the prospect might go cold.

Do you wait 3 days to call after an excellent meeting? A day? A week?

Establishing a client relationship is much like dating. You don't want to appear too zealous, but you don't want to be excessively relaxed either.

It's essential we come across as professional and confident. If we look needy or over-eager, we'll scare business away (and who needs that?). Following-up with prospects is a crucial tool we must use to our advantage; however, it must be utilized in a wise and measured way. Here are a few tips for great follow-up:

1. Ask for their timeline

If you know the timeline, you are able to gauge your reaction. For instance, if you know a person isn't planning to begin for a couple of months, you won't worry when your prospect isn't responding at once to your proposal. On the other hand, a more rushed time table calls for a more immediate reply on your part.

The greatest issue, I my opinion, is when your prospect states "there's no rush, we can complete this whenever." Without being pushy, finalize a time to meet again and put it in your calendar. It will help keep both of you accountable, and keep the momentum going. Regardless what, make certain to call or email within twenty-four hours of meeting. Thank them for their time and the opportunity.

2. Ask if your prospect would like to get your email newsletter

A first-class way to maintain consistent contact with your leads is through an email newsletter. If you don't have one, consider making one (it's an excellent way to promote your business and build "expert status" while providing value to your prospects and customers). If your fresh lead is on the fence, receiving your e-zine will at least remind them you're alive. At most, it will exhibit your talent, expertise, and (maybe) convince them to do business with you.

Bear in mind, inboxes are inundated with unsolicited e-mails and spam. Make certain to get permission before you send a mass email to anyone. Additionally, supply useful, practical information your customers might use. If you're simply marketing at individuals, they'll get annoyed. I find that about one email newsletter a month does an effective job. Naturally, if you have time, you might send letters more frequently.

3. Send off a thank-you note

Sure, you sent an email thank you and even made a phone call. However, nothing beats a good old fashion thank you note sent via the Postal System. Somehow, being able to decipher handwriting and feel a card in your hands simply makes you feel special. If you wish to make an impact, make your prospects feel like they're important. Send them a hand-written note inside a week of meeting. They'll love it.

4. Find a relevant, interesting article and send it

This doesn't have to be an extravagant gesture. If you find a blog post your prospect would find intriguing, send them a link.

Be creative here. To make this gesture personal, make a mental note of personal details about your lead when you're shooting the breeze with them. Do they have children? Do they like to golf? If you remember these personal details, you're more likely to produce an impression. People do business with individuals they like. Make yourself likable, and memorable, by being thoughtful.

Remember, establishing business relationships is much like dating: you have to put yourself out there, you need to take an active interest in your people, and you need to ask for a second date (meeting). The lesson? Follow-up. You'll produce a good impression and develop the sort of client relationships that will ensure your business success.

.

Chapter 5:

About Your Target Market

Synopsis

Interview some individuals in your market by asking: What is working well for you today?

- What are your top 3 hardships?

- What are the 3 things you want most?

- What are you learning about today?

- What is missing for you?

Tailor your services to supply solutions based on their answers. Practice discussing a bulleted list of particular benefits that you offer them. Never discuss vague concepts like helping them accomplish goals and fulfill their dreams. These have no selling power.

Things You Have To Know

The most successful small businesses recognize that only a limited number of people will buy their product or service or sign on. The task then becomes ascertaining, as closely as possible, exactly who those people are, and 'targeting' the business's marketing efforts and dollars towards them.

You, too, may build a better, stronger business, by identifying and serving a particular customer group - your target market.

Among the first things you have to do is to refine your product or service so that you're not attempting to be 'all things to all people.' Become a specialist!

Following, you need to comprehend that people purchase products or services or sign on for 3 basic reasons:

- To meet basic needs.

- To resolve problems.

- To make themselves feel great.

You'll need to find which of those categories your product or service is the solution to, and be geared up to market it accordingly.

Your product or service may fit more than one category, also.

The following step in producing an effective marketing technique is to zero in on your target market.

First of all, is your product international or national in range? Or is it more probable that you'll sell it primarily in your own area or community?

Let's suppose that your primary market is local or regional, and that you live in an area with a population of 35,000 people. The first things you'll have to do is research the 'demographics' of your area, and divide it into market sections:

- Age: youngsters, teens, young, middle, aged

- Sex: male, female

- Education: senior high, college, university

- Revenue: low, medium, high

- Marital status: single, married, split up

- Ethnic and/or spiritual background

- Family life cycle: recently married, married for years, with or without youngsters.

This data ought to be available to you through your local town hall, library, or Chamber of Commerce - and the more detail you may get, the better.

Following, you have to segment the market as much as conceivable utilizing 'psychographics' as your guide:

- Life-style: conservative, exciting, trendy, frugal

- Socio-economic class: lower, middle, upper

- Belief: easily led or opinionated

- Actions and interests: sports, fitness, shopping, books

- Mental attitude and beliefs: environmentalist, security conscious.

If you are a business-to-business company, you'll likewise have to think about the kinds of industries available to you, and their number of employees, yearly sales volume, location, and company stability. Additionally, you might wish to discover how they buy: seasonally, locally, only in volume, who makes the choices? It's crucial to note that businesses, unlike people, buy products or services for 3 reasons only: to better revenue, to sustain the status quo, or to minify expenses. If you fill one or more of these corporate needs, you may have found a target market.

Lots of times prospective leads don't know about your company, or can't tell the difference between your company and others. It's your job, once you realize who your best leads are, to 'target' the group that you've identified - even if you have rivalry.

Additionally, you may decide, utilizing the example above, that you'd likewise like to extend your target market to include women a bit older. If you go back to the basic reasons why people buy goods or services or sign on, and may find ways to target your efforts to that age bracket, you may be successful in capturing a greater share of the market!

On the other hand, what if you 'narrowed down' your product or service and then researched your target market, only to find that there are likely less than 75 people who will be interested in what you have?

First off, if those 75 are corporate leads who will spend 100s on your product or service yearly, then you've nothing to fear. But if those 75 are only going to produce 10 people who like your product or service - then you have to go 'back to the drawing board' of designing your business and possibly determining a wider target market - but at least you're armed with all the data you need to begin again, or go in another direction.

Really - there's a market, and a target market, for everything.

If you don't think so, think about snuggies?

Wrapping Up

I've lost count how many times I've read and heard of celebrity marriages failing. Not that I care , it just seems unusual that we frequently see movie and TV stars as unflawed individuals, living the fairy tale life of riches and glamour. I guess we all have to quit sticking our heads in the sand and confront reality.

There are a lot of ways to lose your sense of confidence despite of how trivial it may be. But whatever occurs, we should all try not to lose our own sense of self.

So what does it take to be a cut above the rest? Here is a recap of the things you are able to improve on.

Know your passion.

Are you drifting through life with little direction - hoping that you'll chance upon happiness, health and prosperity? Identify your life passion or mission statement and you'll have your own unequalled compass that will lead you to your truth every time.

This may appear tricky initially when you feel you're at a dead end. But there's always a way to turn things around and you're able to make a big difference in your life.

Understand your values.

What do you value most? Make a list of your top five values. A couple of examples are security, freedom, loved ones, spiritual development, and learning.

As you set your goals for this year - check your goals against your values. If the goal doesn't line up with any of your top 5 values - you may want to reconsider it or revise it.

Understand your needs.

Unmet needs might keep you from living genuinely. Take care of yourself. Do you have a need to be acknowledged, to be correct, to be in command, to be loved? There are so many individuals who live their lives without realizing their aspirations and most of them wind up being stressed or even depressed for that matter. List your top 4 needs and get them met before it's too late!

Understand your passions.

You know who you are and what you truly like in life. Obstacles like doubt and lack of exuberance will only hinder you, but won't derail your chance to become the individual you ought to be. Express yourself and honor the individuals who have inspired you to become the very individual you wanted to be.

Live from the inside out.

Better your awareness of your inner wisdom by regularly reflecting in silence. Commune with nature. Breathe deeply to calm your distracted mind. For most of us it's difficult to even find the peace and quiet we want even in our own household.

In my case I frequently just sit in a dimly lit room and play some classical music. There's sound, yes, but music does soothe.

Observe your strengths.

What are your favorable traits? What special talents do you have? List 3 - if you bog down, ask those closest to you to help describe these. Are you inventive, witty, and good with your hands? Discover ways to express your genuine self through your strengths. You are able to better your self-confidence when you are able to share what you know to other people.

Serve others.

When you live genuinely, you may find that you develop an interrelated sense of being. When you're true to whom you are, living your passion and giving of your talents to the world around you, you repay in service what you came to share with other people -your spirit - your essence. Sharing your gift with those close to you is so rewarding.

Confidence is indeed one type of work that's worth it. It shouldn't always be inside you. The difference lies inside ourselves and how much we wish to change for the better. Remember that confidence is essential to get your prospects to pay attention to what you are saying and to get them to take action.

www.ingramcontent.com/pod-product-compliance
Lightning Source LLC
LaVergne TN
LVHW021328200726
843509LV00014B/2435